w o k

THE ESSENTIAL KITCHEN

w o k

VICKI LILEY

contents

All about the wok 6

Cooking in a wok 10

Seasoning and cleaning a wok 12

Appetizers and Entrées 14

Beer battered prawns with mango salsa • Peanut and chili bundles
• Shrimp and avocado salad with crispy wontons • Steamed shrimp dumplings
• Mini crab spring rolls • Cilantro shrimp toasts • Fried chicken wontons

Soups 28

Coconut and vegetable soup • Carrot, coconut and ginger soup • Miso with scallops and ginger
• Chicken broth with dumplings • Mushroom and chicken soup

Rice and Noodles 38

Nasi goreng • Steamed rice-and-pork balls • Chili fried rice • Fried noodles with pork
• Salmon laksa • Noodles with baked vegetables • Ginger-coconut rice

Seafood 52

Braised shrimp in ginger-coconut sauce • Stir-fried octopus with long beans and snow peas
• Spicy snapper with parsnip chips • Scallops with arugula pesto and sweet potato purée
• Stir-fried chili-lime shrimp • Fish fillets with coconut rice parcels and tomato-cilantro relish

Beef and Pork 64

Fried pork in endive • Pork and nectarine stir-fry • Pork and lime patties • Red curry beef
• Beef stir-fry with Chinese greens • Dry beef curry with sweet potato

Chicken and Duck 76

Duck with long beans • Chili chicken and vegetables • Deep-fried chicken wings
• Green chicken curry • Crispy wontons with duck • Chicken chow mein

Vegetables 88

Black-eyed pea and sugar snap stir-fry • Butternut squash and lentil salad
• Tofu and vegetable stir-dry • Bell peppers and mushrooms with noodles • Steamed vegetable buns

Desserts 98

Lime and coconut pudding with lime-ginger syrup • Spicy fruit salad
• Polenta pudding with mango sauce • Rose water doughnuts

Glossary 106

Index 109

Guide to weights and measures 111

w o k

ALL ABOUT THE
wok

The word *wok* simply means "cooking vessel" in Cantonese — an indication of how versatile and, indeed, indispensable this piece of equipment is for Asian cooks. Its shape, which has remained unchanged for centuries, was originally dictated by the Chinese stove. The stove had an opening in the top into which the round-bottomed wok securely fit.

A wok is a wonderful and practical addition to the contemporary kitchen. The shape accommodates small or large quantities of ingredients and allows control over how they are cooked. The large cooking surface evenly and efficiently conducts and holds heat, making a wok especially well suited for stir-frying, the quick-cooking technique used frequently in many Asian cuisines. Although the wok is usually associated with stir-frying, there are few cooking methods for which it cannot be used and few ingredients that cannot be cooked in it, whether a recipe is Asian or Western in style.

Of the many woks available, all are basically bowl shaped with gently sloping sides. Some have looped handles on opposite sides; others have a long wooden handle on one side. Woks were traditionally made from cast iron and therefore were quite heavy. They are now available in many different materials and finishes. Carbon or rolled steel is one of the best materials. Nonstick woks are easy to clean but may not promote browning of foods as thoroughly as those made of rolled or carbon steel. Other options include stainless steel woks and electric woks, which may not reach temperatures as high as those of cast iron or carbon steel. Round-bottomed woks work best on gas stoves. A stand may be necessary to provide stability; the best choice is a stand with large perforations that promote good heat circulation. Flat-bottomed woks are suited for electric stove tops because they sit directly and securely on the heating element.

Woks are available in a range of sizes. A wok with a diameter of 14 inches (35 cm) is a versatile size appropriate for the recipes in this book and for other dishes that yield four to six servings. A number of utensils go hand in hand with wok cooking: a lid, a bamboo steamer, a spatula and a slotted spoon.

A SELECTION OF WOKS AND UTENSILS

CAST IRON WOK

NONSTICK WOKS

ELECTRIC WOK

STAINLESS STEEL WOK

TYPES OF WOKS

CARBON STEEL WOK

Stir-frying

This technique uses little fat and retains the fresh flavor, color and texture of ingredients. Meat, poultry, seafood, noodles and vegetables are cooked quickly; stirring them constantly helps ensure uniform doneness. The success of stir-frying depends on having all the ingredients ready before cooking starts.

Deep-frying

The wok is ideal for deep-frying as it uses less oil than a deep fryer and can accommodate ingredients without crowding. Make sure the wok is secure on its stand or heating element before adding the oil. Pour the oil into the wok and heat until it reaches 375°F (190°C) on a deep-frying thermometer or until a cube of bread sizzles and turns golden when dropped into the hot oil.

Steaming

This method cooks foods by moist heat supplied by steadily boiling water. A bamboo steamer set over but not touching simmering water in a wok is ideal for cooking buns, dumplings, fish, vegetables and puddings. Half fill a wok with water (the steamer should not touch the water) and bring to a boil. Arrange the food to be cooked in the steamer, cover, place the steamer in the wok and steam for the required time, adding more water to the wok when necessary. Lift the steamer off the wok and carefully remove the food from the steamer.

Boiling

A wok can serve as a saucepan, a frying pan and a stewing pot, suitable for simmering a delicate coconut sauce, boiling vegetables, simmering a soup or reducing a sauce.

Braising

Meat or seafood can be browned to seal in the juices. Once liquid is added, the wok can be covered for slow simmering.

STIR-FRYING

DEEP-FRYING

STEAMING

BOILING

BRAISING

Woks of carbon steel or rolled steel, the popular inexpensive vessels sold in Asian stores, are coated with a thin film of lacquer to prevent rusting. The film needs to be removed before a wok can be used. The best way to do this is to place the wok on the stove top, fill with cold water and add 2 tablespoons baking soda (bicarbonate of soda). Bring to a boil and boil rapidly for 15 minutes. Drain and scrub off the coating with a nylon pad. Repeat the process if any coating remains. Then rinse and dry the wok. It is now ready to be seasoned.

Carbon steel, rolled steel and cast iron woks require seasoning before use, which creates a smooth surface that keeps food from sticking to it and prevents it from discoloring. To season a wok, place over low heat. Have paper towels and vegetable oil handy. When the wok is hot, carefully wipe it with an oiled paper towel. Repeat the process with fresh towels until they come away clean, without any trace of color.

A seasoned wok should not be scrubbed clean with detergent after cooking. Instead, use hot water and a sponge or nylon pad. Dry the wok well after washing and store in a dry, well-ventilated place. Long periods without use can cause the oil coating on the wok to become rancid. Using a wok is the best way to prevent this from occurring.

Beer-battered prawns with mango salsa

MANGO SALSA

1 mango, peeled, pitted and chopped

$^1/_2$ cup (2 oz/60 g) chopped scallions
  (shallots/spring onions)

$^1/_2$ small red chili pepper, seeded and chopped

3 tablespoons lime juice

2 teaspoons Asian sesame oil

$^1/_2$ cup ($^3/_4$ oz/20 g) chopped fresh basil

ground pepper to taste

BATTERED PRAWNS

$1^1/_2$ cups ($7^1/_2$ oz/235 g) all-purpose (plain) flour

1 teaspoon baking powder (bicarbonate of soda)

1 teaspoon salt

$^1/_2$ teaspoon red pepper flakes

1 teaspoon brown sugar

$1^3/_4$ cups (14 fl oz/440 ml) beer

3 cups (24 fl oz/750 ml) vegetable oil for deep-frying

20 jumbo shrimp (king prawns), peeled and
  deveined, tails intact

lime wedges for serving

To make salsa, combine mango, scallions, chili pepper, lime juice, sesame oil, basil and ground pepper in bowl. Mix well and set aside.

To make prawns, sift flour, baking powder and salt into bowl. Stir in red pepper flakes and sugar. Pour in beer and mix with wooden spoon until batter is smooth.

Heat oil in wok until it reaches 375°F (190°C) on deep-frying thermometer or until small bread cube dropped in oil sizzles and turns golden. Dip prawns, one at a time, into batter, allow excess to drain off and carefully drop in hot oil. Deep-fry until golden, 30–60 seconds. Using slotted spoon, remove from wok and drain on paper towels. Continue until all prawns are cooked.

Serve prawns hot with lime wedges and mango salsa.

Serves 6–8 as appetizer, 4 as entrée

BEER-BATTERED PRAWNS WITH MANGO SALSA

Peanut and chili bundles

1 cup (5¹/₂ oz/165 g) unsalted roasted peanuts

1 small red chili pepper, seeded and finely chopped

8 scallions (shallots/green onions), finely chopped

¹/₄ cup (¹/₃ oz/10 g) chopped fresh cilantro (fresh coriander)

¹/₂ cup (4 fl oz/125 ml) lemon juice

¹/₂ cup (1 oz/30 g) fresh white bread crumbs

1 teaspoon superfine (caster) sugar

24 wonton wrappers

4 cups (32 fl oz/1 L) vegetable oil for deep-frying

lime wedges and Thai sweet chili sauce or soy sauce for serving

Place peanuts in food processor or blender and process until fine. Transfer to bowl. Add chili pepper, scallions, cilantro, lemon juice, bread crumbs and sugar. Mix well.

Place wonton wrappers on work surface and cover with damp towel to prevent them from drying out. Working with one wrapper at a time, place 1 teaspoon peanut filling in middle. Brush edges with water, gather edges together and twist to seal. Set aside, covered with plastic wrap. Repeat with remaining wonton wrappers.

Heat oil in wok until it reaches 375°F (190°C) on deep-frying thermometer or until small bread cube cropped in oil sizzles and turns golden. Working in batches, add wontons and fry until golden, 1–2 minutes. Using slotted spoon, remove from wok and drain on paper towels.

Serve bundles hot with lime wedges and with Thai sweet chili sauce or soy sauce for dipping.

Serves 8–10 as appetizer, 6 as entrée

PEANUT AND CHILI BUNDLES

Shrimp and avocado salad with crispy wontons

GRAPEFRUIT DRESSING

$^1/_4$ cup (2 fl oz/60 ml) grapefruit juice

$^1/_4$ cup (2 fl oz/60 ml) olive oil

2 teaspoons palm sugar or brown sugar

1 tablespoon white wine vinegar

1 teaspoon peeled and grated fresh ginger

SALAD

2 tablespoons vegetable oil, plus 3 cups
   (24 fl oz/750 ml) oil for deep-frying

3 cloves garlic, crushed

20 jumbo shrimp (king prawns), peeled and
   deveined, tails intact

12 wonton wrappers

$^1/_2$ avocado, peeled, pitted and chopped

1 tomato, chopped

$^1/_2$ red onion, chopped

$^1/_4$ cup ($^1/_3$ oz/10 g) chopped fresh cilantro
   (fresh coriander)

To make dressing, place grapefruit juice, olive oil, sugar, vinegar and ginger in screw-top jar. Shake well to combine and set aside.

To make salad, in wok over medium-high heat, warm 2 tablespoons vegetable oil. Add garlic and stir-fry until aromatic, about 1 minute. Raise heat to high, add shrimp and stir-fry until shrimp change color, 3–4 minutes. Remove from wok and drain on paper towels. Set aside to cool.

Heat 3 cups (24 fl oz/750 ml) oil in wok until it reaches 375°F (190°C) on deep-frying thermometer or until small bread cube dropped in oil sizzles and turns golden. Working in batches, add wonton wrappers and deep-fry until golden and crisp, about 1 minute. Using slotted spoon or tongs, remove from wok and drain on paper towels. Set aside to cool.

In bowl, combine avocado, tomato, onion and cilantro. Add shrimp and grapefruit dressing and gently stir until well combined. Cover and allow to stand for 10 minutes for flavors to develop.

Place one wonton on each plate and top with salad. Add another wonton and layer of salad. Top with third wonton. Serve immediately.

Serves 4

Steamed shrimp dumplings

8 oz (250 g) jumbo shrimp (king prawns), peeled
and deveined

2 tablespoons finely chopped drained canned
water chestnuts

2 scallions (shallots/spring onions), chopped,
plus shredded scallions for serving

1 tablespoon light soy sauce, plus soy sauce for
dipping

1/2 teaspoon Asian sesame oil

12 wonton wrappers

Place shrimp in food processor and process until smooth. Transfer to bowl. Add water chestnuts, chopped scallions, 1 tablespoon soy sauce and sesame oil. Mix until well combined.

Place wonton wrappers on work surface and cover with damp kitchen towel to prevent them from drying out. Working with one wrapper at a time, lay it on work surface and place 1 teaspoon shrimp filling in middle. Brush edges with water, gather edges together and twist to seal. Set aside, covered with plastic wrap. Repeat with remaining wonton wrappers.

Line bamboo steamer with parchment (baking) paper. Half fill wok with water (steamer should not touch water) and bring water to boil. Arrange filled wontons in steamer, cover and place steamer over boiling water. Steam for 20 minutes, adding more water to wok when necessary. Lift steamer off wok and carefully remove dumplings from steamer.

Arrange dumplings on individual plates and garnish with shredded scallions. Serve warm with soy sauce for dipping.

Serves 6 as appetizer, 3 or 4 as entrée

STEAMED SHRIMP DUMPLINGS

Mini crab spring rolls

DIPPING SAUCE

1 tablespoon fish sauce

3 tablespoons lime juice

1 scallion (shallot/spring onion), finely chopped

1 small red chili pepper, seeded and chopped

1 teaspoon palm sugar or brown sugar

1 tablespoon finely chopped fresh cilantro
  (fresh coriander)

1 tablespoon rice wine vinegar

$1/2$ small cucumber, peeled, seeded and finely
  chopped

CRAB SPRING ROLLS

2 teaspoons vegetable oil, plus 4 cups
  (32 fl oz/1 L) oil for deep-frying

1 bunch bok choy, trimmed and shredded

4 kaffir lime leaves, finely shredded, or 1 teaspoon
  grated lime zest

8 oz (250 g) fresh or drained canned crabmeat

2 tablespoons chopped fresh cilantro (fresh
  coriander)

1 tablespoon lime juice

18–20 thawed frozen mini spring roll wrappers,
  about $4^{1}/_{2}$-in (11.5-cm) square

2 teaspoons cornstarch (cornflour) mixed with
  2 tablespoons water

To make dipping sauce, combine fish sauce, lime juice, scallion, chili pepper, sugar, cilantro, vinegar and cucumber. Stir to combine and set aside.

To make spring rolls, in wok over high heat, warm 2 teaspoons vegetable oil. Add bok choy and stir-fry until softened, about 1 minute. Remove from heat, place in bowl and allow to cool completely. Stir in kaffir lime leaves, crabmeat, cilantro and lime juice. Mix until well combined.

Separate spring roll wrappers, place on work surface and cover with damp kitchen towel to prevent them from drying out. Working with one wrapper at a time, lay it on work surface and place 1 tablespoon filling in middle. Using fingertips, moisten edges with cornstarch and water mixture. Roll up diagonally to enclose filling, tucking in edges. Seal with cornstarch and water mixture. Set aside, covered with plastic wrap. Repeat with remaining wrappers.

Heat 4 cups (32 fl oz/1 l) vegetable oil in wok until it reaches 375°F (190°C) on deep-frying thermometer or until small bread cube dropped in oil sizzles and turns golden. Working in batches, add rolls and fry until golden, about 1 minute. Using slotted spoon, remove from wok and drain on paper towels.

Serve hot, accompanied with dipping sauce.

Serves 6–8 as appetizer, 3 or 4 as entrée

MINI CRAB SPRING ROLLS

Cilantro shrimp toasts

1 lb (500 g) jumbo shrimp (king prawns), peeled and deveined

4 French shallots, coarsely chopped

1 lemongrass stalk, bruised and coarsely chopped

2 cloves garlic

1 egg white

2 teaspoons fish sauce

1 small red chili pepper, seeded and chopped

1 teaspoon lemon juice

4 kaffir lime leaves, shredded, or 1 teaspoon grated lime zest

2 tablespoons finely chopped fresh cilantro (fresh coriander)

35–40 slices white bread

2 tablespoons sesame seeds

3 cups (24 fl oz/750 ml) vegetable oil for deep-frying

Place shrimp, shallots, lemongrass, garlic, egg white, fish sauce, chili pepper and lemon juice in food processor and process until smooth. Transfer to bowl. Stir in kaffir lime leaves or lime zest and cilantro. Mix until well combined.

Using star-shaped or round cookie cutter 3 inches (7.5 cm) in diameter, cut one star or round from each bread slice (reserve leftover bread for making crumbs). Spread 1 scant teaspoon shrimp mixture on each bread shape. Sprinkle with sesame seeds and press gently into shrimp mixture.

Heat oil in large wok until it reaches 375°F (190°C) on deep-frying thermometer or until small bread cube dropped in oil sizzles and turns golden. Working in batches, add toasts and fry until golden on both sides, 1–2 minutes. Using slotted spoon, remove from wok and drain on paper towels.

Arrange toasts on serving platter or individual plates and serve hot.

Serves 10–12 as appetizer

CILANTRO SHRIMP TOASTS

Fried chicken wontons

1 tablespoon vegetable oil, plus 4 cups
  (32 fl oz/1 L) oil for deep-frying

1 onion, chopped

1 clove garlic, crushed

8 oz (250 g) ground (minced) chicken

2 tablespoon chunky peanut butter

1 tablespoon Thai sweet chili sauce

1 tablespoon lemon juice

1/4 cup (1/3 oz/10 g) chopped fresh cilantro
  (fresh coriander)

48 round wonton wrappers

chili oil for serving

In wok over medium-high heat, warm 1 tablespoon vegetable oil. Add onion and garlic and stir-fry until softened, 1–2 minutes. Add chicken and stir-fry until chicken changes color. Remove from heat. Add peanut butter, chili sauce, lemon juice and cilantro. Allow to cool completely.

Place wonton wrappers on work surface and cover with damp kitchen towel to prevent them from drying out. Working with one wrapper at a time, lay it on work surface and place 1 heaping teaspoon chicken filling in middle. Brush edges with water. Place another wonton wrapper on top and firmly press edges together. Set aside, covered with plastic wrap. Repeat with remaining wonton wrappers.

Heat 4 cups (32 fl oz/1 L) vegetable oil in large wok until it reaches 375°F (190°C) on deep-frying thermometer or until small bread cube dropped in oil sizzles and turns golden. Working in batches, add wontons and fry until golden on both sides, 1–2 minutes. Using a slotted spoon, remove from wok and drain on paper towels.

Serve wontons hot, accompanied with chili oil.

Serves 10–12 as appetizer, 6–8 as entrée

Tip

If round wonton wrappers are unavailable, purchase square wrappers and cut into rounds.

FRIED CHICKEN WONTONS

Coconut and vegetable soup

1 tablespoon vegetable oil

$^1/_4$ teaspoon shrimp paste

1 clove garlic, crushed

$^1/_4$ cup ($^1/_3$ oz/10 g) chopped fresh cilantro
(fresh coriander) stems

4 scallions (shallots/green onions) chopped

3 cups (24 fl oz/750 ml) chicken or vegetable broth

1 cup (8 fl oz/250 ml) coconut milk

1 tablespoon fish sauce

2 cups (6 oz/180 g) finely shredded green cabbage

12 snow peas (mange-touts), trimmed and sliced
crosswise

1 carrot, peeled and julienned

1 cup (3 oz/90 g) small broccoli florets

3 tablespoons lime juice

2 teaspoons sambal oelek

1 tablespoon chopped fresh cilantro (fresh
coriander)

In wok over medium heat, warm oil. Add shrimp paste, garlic, cilantro stems and scallions and stir-fry until softened, about 1 minute. Add broth, coconut milk and fish sauce. Bring to boil, then reduce heat to low. Add cabbage, snow peas, carrot and broccoli. Simmer, uncovered, until vegetables are just tender, about 10 minutes.

Stir in lime juice, sambal oelek and cilantro.

Serve hot, ladled into individual bowls.

Serves 4

COCONUT AND VEGETABLE SOUP

Carrot, coconut and ginger soup

1 tablespoon vegetable oil

1 teaspoon Asian sesame oil

1 small red chili pepper, seeded and chopped

4 cloves garlic, crushed

3 teaspoons peeled and grated fresh ginger

2 onions, chopped

2 lb (1 kg) carrots, peeled and sliced

1 teaspoon ground cumin

1 teaspoon ground turmeric

4 cups (32 fl oz/1 L) coconut milk

2 cups (16 fl oz/500 ml) vegetable or chicken broth

salt and ground pepper to taste

fresh tarragon leaves for serving

In wok over medium heat, warm vegetable and sesame oils. Add chili pepper, garlic and ginger and stir-fry until aromatic, about 1 minute. Add onions, carrots, cumin and turmeric and stir-fry until onions are softened, about 2 minutes.

Pour in coconut milk and broth. Bring to boil, reduce heat to low and simmer, uncovered, until carrots are tender, 12–15 minutes. Remove from heat.

Working in batches, ladle soup into food processor or blender and process until smooth. Return to wok and heat through for 2 minutes. Taste and season with salt and pepper.

To serve, ladle into individual bowls and garnish with tarragon leaves.

Serves 4

CARROT, COCONUT AND GINGER SOUP

Miso with scallops and ginger

8 oz (250 g) scallops, cut in half if large

$^{1}/_{4}$ cup (1 oz/30 g) peeled and shredded fresh
  ginger

$^{1}/_{4}$ cup ($^{1}/_{3}$ oz/10 g) chopped fresh cilantro
  (fresh coriander)

$1^{1}/_{2}$ cups (12 fl oz/375 ml) water

1 lemongrass stalk, bruised and finely chopped

4 kaffir lime leaves, finely shredded, or 1 teaspoon
  grated lime zest

2 tablespoon red miso paste

1 teaspoon lime juice

Place scallops, ginger, cilantro, water and lemongrass in wok. Bring to boil. Reduce heat, cover and simmer until scallops are opaque, 1–2 minutes.

Remove from heat and pour through strainer into bowl. Reserve liquid. Set scallops and spices aside and keep warm.

Measure liquid and add water to make 4 cups (32 fl oz/1 L). Return to wok and bring to boil. Stir in miso and lime juice, reduce heat and simmer for 3 minutes.

To serve, divide scallops among individual plates. Ladle miso into small bowls.

Serves 4

MISO WITH SCALLOPS AND GINGER

Chicken broth with dumplings

2 tablespoons butter, softened

1 egg, beaten

1 cup (2 oz/60 g) fresh white bread crumbs

2 teaspoons peeled and grated fresh ginger, plus
3 thin slices ginger

2 tablespoons chopped fresh cilantro
(fresh coriander)

4 cups (32 fl oz/1 L) chicken broth

2 lemongrass stalks, bruised and chopped

1 small red chili pepper, seeded and chopped

$^1/_4$ cup (1 oz/30 g) shredded scallions
(shallots/green onions)

In bowl, combine butter, egg, bread crumbs, grated ginger and cilantro. Using wooden spoon or fingertips, mix until well combined. Set dumpling mixture aside.

Place chicken broth, ginger slices, lemongrass and chili pepper in large wok. Bring to boil, reduce heat to low and simmer, uncovered, for 10 minutes. Strain through fine-mesh strainer into bowl. Discard solids. Return broth to wok and keep warm.

Place 3 cups (24 fl oz/750 ml) water into another wok or saucepan. Bring to boil and reduce heat so water gently simmers. Working in batches, drop 1 heaping teaspoon dumpling mixture, into simmering water. Cook until firm, 2–3 minutes. Using slotted spoon, remove from simmering water. Repeat with remaining mixture.

Ladle hot broth into individual bowls. Divide dumplings among bowls and garnish with shredded scallions. Serve immediately.

Serves 4

Mushroom and chicken soup

4 Chinese dried mushrooms

4 cups (32 fl oz/1 L) chicken broth

2 cloves garlic, crushed

1 teaspoon peeled and grated ginger

1 tablespoon rice vinegar

2 teaspoons palm sugar or brown sugar

1 chicken fillet, about 5 oz (150 g), thinly sliced

6 scallions (shallots/spring onions), chopped

2 lemongrass stalks, bruised and sliced

1 small red chili pepper, seeded and chopped

Place mushrooms in small bowl, add boiling water to cover and allow to stand until softened, 10–15 minutes. Drain and squeeze excess liquid from mushrooms. Thinly slice, discarding thick stems.

Place broth, garlic, ginger, vinegar and sugar in wok. Bring to boil, reduce heat to low and simmer, uncovered, for 5 minutes. Stir in sliced mushrooms, chicken, scallions, lemongrass and chili pepper. Simmer until chicken is opaque, about 15 minutes.

Serve hot, ladled into bowls.

Serves 4

MUSHROOM AND CHICKEN SOUP

noodles

Nasi goreng

3 teaspoons peeled and grated fresh ginger

1 teaspoon ground turmeric

1 teaspoon shrimp paste

2 teaspoons chili sauce

3 tablespoons peanut oil

1 onion, chopped

3 cloves garlic, crushed

$^1/_2$ red bell pepper (capsicum), seeded and
   chopped

1 celery stalk, chopped

1 carrot, peeled and chopped

$^1/_2$ cup ($2^1/_2$ oz/75 g) thawed frozen peas

4 oz (125 g) Chinese barbecue pork, chopped

1 cup (4 oz/125 g) fresh bean sprouts, rinsed

1 cup (3 oz/90 g) shredded bok choy

4 cups (20 oz/625 g) cold cooked jasmine rice

4 oz (125 g) cooked shrimp (prawns), peeled and
   deveined, tails intact

$^1/_4$ cup (2 fl oz/60 ml) coconut milk

2 tablespoons light soy sauce

Combine ginger, turmeric, shrimp paste and chili sauce in small bowl. Mix to form paste. Set aside.

In wok over medium-high heat, warm peanut oil. Add onion and garlic and stir-fry until onion softens, about 1 minute. Stir in spice paste, bell pepper, celery, carrot, peas, pork, bean sprouts and bok choy. Raise heat to high and stir-fry until vegetables soften slightly, 3–4 minutes. Add rice and shrimp and stir-fry until rice is heated through, about 3 minutes. Combine coconut milk and soy sauce, add to wok and stir until evenly combined and mixture is hot.

Spoon into individual bowls. Serve hot as main course or as accompaniment to other stir-fried dishes.

Serves 4–6

Steamed rice-and-pork balls

1 cup (7 oz/220 g) short-grain white rice

1 lb (500 g) ground (minced) pork

4 scallions (shallots/spring onions), chopped

2 tablespoons drained canned water chestnuts

1 tablespoon oyster sauce

2 tablespoons fresh cilantro (fresh coriander) leaves

2 cloves garlic, crushed

1 tablespoon peeled and grated fresh ginger

2 teaspoons light soy sauce, plus soy sauce for serving

2 teaspoons Thai sweet chili sauce, plus chili sauce for serving

Place rice in bowl. Cover with cold water and allow to stand for 30 minutes. Drain, spread out on paper towel–lined tray and allow to dry.

In bowl, combine pork, scallions, water chestnuts, oyster sauce, cilantro, garlic, ginger, 2 teaspoons soy sauce and 2 teaspoons chili sauce. Using moistened hands, mix until well combined. Shape into 20 small balls. Roll each ball in rice until well coated.

Half fill wok with water (steamer should not touch water) and bring to boil. Working in batches, arrange balls in steamer, allowing space for rice to expand. Cover, place steamer over boiling water and steam for 30 minutes, adding more water to wok when necessary. Lift steamer from wok and carefully remove balls from steamer.

Serve warm, with soy sauce or chili sauce for dipping.

Serves 4

STEAMED RICE-AND-PORK BALLS

Chili fried rice

3 tablespoons vegetable oil

1 onion, chopped

1 small red chili pepper, seeded and chopped

1 tablespoon red curry paste

5 oz (150 g) pork fillet, thinly sliced

12 jumbo shrimp (king prawns), peeled and
deveined, tails intact

4 cups (20 oz/625 g) cooked white rice, chilled

2 eggs, beaten

1 tablespoon fish sauce

$^1/_2$ cup ($1^1/_2$ oz/45 g) chopped scallions
(shallots/spring onions)

$^1/_3$ cup ($^1/_2$ oz/15 g) chopped fresh cilantro
(fresh coriander)

3 small red chili flowers (optional; see note)

In wok over medium-high heat, warm oil. Add onion and chili pepper and stir-fry until onion is softened, about 2 minutes. Stir in curry paste and cook for 1 minute. Add pork and stir-fry until pork changes color, 3–4 minutes. Add shrimp and stir-fry until shrimp change color, about 3 minutes. Add rice and stir-fry until rice is coated with oil.

Push rice to one side of wok. Add beaten eggs and allow to partially set without stirring, then mix with rice. Stir in fish sauce, scallions and cilantro.

Serve hot as main course or as accompaniment to stir-fried dishes. Garnish with chili flowers, if desired.

Serves 4

Note

To make red chili flower, using sharp knife, make closely spaced cuts along the length of small red chili pepper, allowing chili to stay attached at stem end. Place in bowl of ice water. Chill until chili curls, about 15 minutes.

CHILI FRIED RICE

Fried noodles with pork

8 oz (250 g) fresh or dried egg noodles

1 tablespoon vegetable oil

1 bunch Chinese broccoli, cut into 3-in (7.5-cm) lengths

8 oz (250 g) Chinese barbecue pork, sliced

$\frac{1}{2}$ cup (5 oz/150 g) chunky peanut butter

2 teaspoon Asian sesame oil

2 tablespoons light soy sauce

2 teaspoons garam masala

3 cloves garlic, crushed

1 small red chili pepper, seeded and chopped

Bring saucepan of water to boil. Add noodles and cook until tender, about 3 minutes for fresh noodles, about 5 minutes for dried noodles. (If using precooked noodles, soak in boiling water for 8–10 minutes.) Drain and keep warm.

In wok over medium-high heat, warm vegetable oil. Add broccoli and pork and stir-fry for 4 minutes. In small bowl, combine peanut butter, sesame oil, soy sauce, garam masala, garlic and chili. Mix until well combined. Add peanut butter mixture and noodles to wok. Raise heat to high and stir-fry until heated through, about 1 minute. Do not overcook.

Serve hot.

Serves 4

FRIED NOODLES WITH PORK

Salmon laksa

6¹/₂ oz (200 g) cellophane (bean thread) noodles

3 small red chili peppers, seeded and chopped

3 cloves garlic

1 piece peeled fresh ginger, about 2¹/₂ in (6 cm)
   long

¹/₂ cup (²/₃ oz/20 g) fresh cilantro (fresh
   coriander) leaves

3 teaspoons vegetable oil

1 teaspoon Asian sesame oil

4 cups (32 fl oz/1 L) coconut milk

3 cups (24 fl oz/750 ml) fish broth or 1¹/₂ cups
   (12 fl oz/375 ml) each clam juice and water

8 oz (250 g) salmon fillet, skin and errant bones
   removed, sliced into 12 thin slices

2 tablespoons lemon juice

1 tablespoon fish sauce

4 scallions (shallots/spring onions), sliced

¹/₄ cup (¹/₄ oz/7 g) fresh mint leaves

Place noodles in bowl and soak in boiling water for 10 minutes. Drain and set aside.

Place chili peppers, garlic, ginger and cilantro in food processor. Process to form smooth paste.

In wok over medium-high heat, warm vegetable and sesame oils. Add spice paste and cook until aromatic, about 1 minute. Add coconut milk and broth or clam juice and water, and bring to boil. Reduce heat to low and simmer, uncovered, for 10 minutes. Add salmon, lemon juice and fish sauce and simmer until salmon is opaque, 2–3 minutes.

To serve, divide noodles among individual bowls. Ladle soup over noodles. Sprinkle each serving with scallions and mint leaves.

Serves 6

SALMON LAKSA

Noodles with baked vegetables

8 oz (250 g) fresh or dried egg noodles or udon
noodles

1 lb (500 g) butternut squash (pumpkin), cut into
1-in (2.5-cm) pieces

2 carrots, peeled and cut into 1-in (2.5-cm) pieces

3 tablespoons vegetable oil

5 cloves garlic, crushed

6½ oz (200 g) zucchini (courgette), cut into
1-in (2.5-cm) pieces

2 onions, chopped

1 cup (8 fl oz/250 ml) coconut milk

¼ cup (⅓ oz/10 g) chopped fresh cilantro
(fresh coriander)

1 small red chili pepper, seeded and chopped

salt and ground pepper to taste

Preheat oven to 400°F (200°C/Gas 6). Bring saucepan of water to boil. Add noodles and cook until tender, about 2½ minutes for fresh udon noodles, about 3 minutes for fresh egg noodles, about 5 minutes for dried egg noodles, 10–12 minutes for dried udon noodles. Drain and set aside.

In baking dish, combine squash, carrots, 2 tablespoons vegetable oil and 3 cloves garlic. Toss to coat vegetables in oil. Bake, uncovered, for 15 minutes. Remove from oven, add zucchini, stir vegetables, return to oven and bake until vegetables are tender, about 15 minutes longer.

In wok over medium-high heat, warm remaining 1 tablespoon vegetable oil. Add onions and remaining 2 cloves garlic and stir-fry until onions soften, 2–3 minutes. Add coconut milk, cilantro and chili pepper. Stir until heated through, 3–4 minutes. Add baked vegetables and noodles. Cook until heated through, 1–2 minutes. Taste and season with salt and pepper.

Divide among individual bowls and serve immediately.

Serves 4

NOODLES WITH BAKED VEGETABLES

Ginger-coconut rice

2 tablespoons vegetable oil

1 teaspoon chili oil

1 onion, chopped

1 red bell pepper (capsicum), seeded and chopped

3 cloves garlic, crushed

3 teaspoons peeled and grated fresh ginger

1 1/2 cups (10 1/2 oz/330 g) short-grain white rice

1 1/2 cups (12 fl oz/375 ml) chicken broth

1 cup (8 fl oz/250 ml) water

1/2 cup (4 fl oz/125 ml) coconut milk

3 scallions (shallots/spring onions)

3 tablespoons chopped fresh cilantro (fresh
   coriander)

2 tablespoons unsweetened shredded coconut,
   toasted

3 tablespoons lemon juice

1/4 cup (1 oz/30 g) unsweetened shredded coconut
   for serving

In wok over medium-high heat, warm vegetable and chili oils. Add onion, bell pepper, garlic and ginger and stir-fry until softened, about 3 minutes. Add rice and stir until well coated with oil, about 2 minutes.

Add broth, water and coconut milk and bring to boil. Reduce heat to low, cover and simmer until all liquid is absorbed and rice is tender, 15–20 minutes. Remove from heat and stir in scallions, cilantro, toasted coconut and lemon juice.

Serve hot, topped with shredded coconut.

Serves 4–6

Note

This ginger-laced rice, which gains a subtle sweetness from both shredded coconut and coconut milk, makes a good accompaniment for Chinese barbecue pork.

Braised shrimp
in ginger-coconut sauce

2 tablespoons peeled and grated fresh ginger

4 cloves garlic, crushed

1 tablespoon ground turmeric

1 small red chili pepper, seeded and chopped

2 tablespoons white vinegar

2 tablespoons peanut oil

2 onions, chopped

1 lb (500 g) jumbo shrimp (king prawns), peeled
   and deveined, tails intact

2 tomatoes, chopped

$^3/_4$ cup (6 fl oz/180 ml) coconut milk

2 teaspoons cracked black pepper

2 tablespoons chopped fresh cilantro (fresh
   coriander)

$^1/_4$ cup ($^1/_4$ oz/7 g) small whole cilantro (coriander
   leaves)

Place ginger, garlic, turmeric, chili pepper and vinegar in food processor or blender. Process to form paste.

In wok over medium-high heat, warm peanut oil. Add onions and spice paste and stir-fry until onions soften, 2–3 minutes. Add shrimp and stir-fry until shrimp change color, 3–4 minutes. Stir in tomatoes and cook until soft, about 2 minutes. Add coconut milk, reduce heat to low, cover and simmer until sauce thickens slightly and shrimp are tender, 6–8 minutes. Stir in pepper and chopped cilantro.

Serve hot, garnished with cilantro leaves.

Serves 4

BRAISED SHRIMP IN GINGER-COCONUT SAUCE

Stir-fried octopus with long beans and snow peas

1 lb (500 g) baby octopus

1 tablespoon light soy sauce

3 tablespoons vegetable oil

1 tablespoon dry sherry

2 cloves garlic, crushed

2 teaspoons grated lime zest

2 tablespoon lime juice

3 small red chili peppers, seeded and halved

5 oz (150 g) long beans, cut into 4-in (10-cm) lengths

4 kaffir lime leaves, shredded, or 1 teaspoon grated lime zest

5 oz (155 g) snow peas (mange-touts), trimmed and sliced crosswise

Working with one octopus at a time, slit open head and remove intestines. Rinse and place in glass or ceramic bowl. In small bowl, combine soy sauce, 1 tablespoon vegetable oil, sherry, garlic, 2 teaspoons lime zest and lime juice. Pour over octopus, cover and refrigerate for 1 hour.

Drain octopus and reserve marinade. In wok over medium heat, warm remaining 2 tablespoons vegetable oil. Add chili peppers and stir-fry until aromatic, 1–2 minutes. Add octopus and stir-fry for 2 minutes. Add beans, lime leaves or lime zest, snow peas and reserved marinade. Stir-fry until vegetables are tender-crisp and octopus is cooked through (do not overcook or octopus will toughen), 1–2 minutes.

Serve hot.

Serves 4

Note

You may like to substitute octopus with 6 x 1 lb (500g) squid bodies. Cut squid tubes in half lengthwise. Cut shallow slashes in a cross-cross pattern on outside of squid and cut squid into $3/4$ inch (2 cm) strips. Marinate and cook as for octopus.

Spicy snapper with parsnip chips

2 teaspoon ground cumin

1 green chili pepper, seeded and sliced

1/2 cup (2/3 oz/20 g) fresh cilantro (fresh coriander) leaves

3 cloves garlic

1 piece peeled fresh ginger, about 1 1/4 in (3 cm)

2 teaspoons garam marsala

4 small snapper, 6–8 oz (180–250 g) each, cleaned

6 cups (48 fl oz/1.5 L) vegetable oil for deep-frying

2 parsnips, peeled

lime wedges for serving

Place cumin, chili pepper, cilantro, garlic, ginger and garam marsala in food processor and process until smooth. Using sharp knife, cut 3 shallow slits in each side of fish. Rub spice mixture into each side. Place on glass or ceramic plate, cover and refrigerate for 1 hour.

Heat vegetable oil in wok until it reaches 375°F (190°C) on deep-frying thermometer or until small bread cube dropped in oil sizzles and turns golden. Add fish, one at a time, and cook, turning once, until golden and crisp on both sides, about 4 minutes. Using tongs and spatula, carefully remove fish from wok and drain on paper towels. Repeat with remaining fish. Keep warm.

Thinly slice parsnips lengthwise, using vegetable peeler. Add slices to wok and cook until golden and crisp, about 1 minute. Using slotted spoon, remove from wok and drain on paper towels.

Arrange fish and parsnip chips on individual plates. Garnish with lime wedge and serve.

Serves 4

Scallops with arugula pesto and sweet potato purée

ARUGULA PESTO

1 bunch arugula (rocket)

¹/₄ cup (1 oz/30 g) pine nuts, toasted

¹/₄ cup (1 oz/30 g) grated parmesan cheese

ground pepper to taste

2 cloves garlic, crushed

¹/₄ cup (2 fl oz/60 ml) extra virgin olive oil

SCALLOPS AND SWEET POTATO PURÉE

1 lb (500 g) sweet potatoes, peeled and cut into
  2-in (5-cm) pieces

2 tablespoons olive oil

3 cloves garlic, crushed

2 tablespoons vegetable oil

1 small red chili pepper, seeded and chopped

1 lb (500 g) scallops, halved if large

1 tablespoon lime juice

lime wedges for serving

To make pesto, place arugula, pine nuts, parmesan cheese, pepper and garlic in food processor. Process until finely chopped. With motor running, gradually pour in olive oil and process until well combined. Set aside.

Half fill saucepan with water. Bring to boil, add sweet potatoes, reduce heat to medium and cook until tender, 10–12 minutes. Drain, transfer to bowl and mash with fork or potato masher. Stir in olive oil and 2 garlic cloves. Set aside and keep warm.

In wok over medium heat, warm vegetable oil. Add chili pepper and remaining garlic clove and stir-fry until aromatic, about 1 minute. Add scallops and stir-fry until tender (do not overcook or scallops will toughen), 2–3 minutes. Remove from heat and stir in lime juice.

To serve, spoon sweet potato purée on individual plates. Top with pesto, then place scallops over pesto. Serve hot, accompanied with lime wedges. Store any leftover pesto in screw-top jar in refrigerator.

Serves 4

Stir-fried chili-lime shrimp

1 lb (500 g) jumbo shrimp (king prawns), peeled
   and deveined, tails intact

pinch of ground chili

$1/_4$ teaspoon ground turmeric

3 tablespoons vegetable oil

3 cloves garlic, crushed

1 small red chili pepper, seeded and chopped

1 teaspoon black mustard seeds

1 tablespoon lime juice

lime wedges for serving

Place shrimp in bowl. Combine ground chili and turmeric and sprinkle over shrimp. Using hands, rub spices into shrimp.

In wok over medium-high heat, warm vegetable oil. Add garlic, chili pepper and mustard seeds and stir-fry until seeds begin to pop, 1–2 minutes. Raise heat to high, add shrimp and stir-fry until shrimp change color and are tender, 3–4 minutes. Remove from heat and stir in lime juice.

Serve hot, accompanied with lime wedges.

Serves 4

Fish fillets with coconut rice parcels and cilantro-tomato relish

CILANTRO-TOMATO RELISH

2 tomatoes, chopped

$^1/_4$ cup ($^1/_3$ oz/10 g) chopped fresh cilantro (fresh coriander)

3 tablespoons lime juice

1 kaffir lime leaf, finely shredded

STEAMED FISH

2 teaspoons peeled and grated ginger

$^1/_4$ teaspoon ground coriander

pinch of ground turmeric

1 small white onion, finely chopped

1 green chili pepper, seeded and chopped

2 tablespoons unsweetened shredded (desiccated) coconut

1 clove garlic, crushed

4 whole cloves

3–4 teaspoons lime juice

4 fish fillets such as perch or monk fish, 4–6 oz (125–180 g) each

COCONUT RICE PARCELS

$^3/_4$ cup (5 oz/150 g) glutinous rice

1 tablespoon peanut oil

1 white onion, chopped

1 teaspoon ground cardamom

1 cup (8 fl oz/250 ml) water

$^1/_2$ cup (4 fl oz/125 ml) coconut milk

$^1/_3$ cup (3 fl oz/90 ml) warm water

4–6 fresh young banana leaves, rinsed and cut into 7-in (18-cm) squares

To make relish, combine tomatoes, cilantro, lime juice and kaffir lime leaves. Mix well and set aside. To make steamed fish, combine ginger, coriander, turmeric, onion, chili pepper, coconut, garlic and cloves in small bowl. Gradually add enough lime juice to form thick paste. If fish fillets have skin, slash skin side several times with sharp knife. Spread spice paste on flesh side of each fillet. Place on glass or ceramic plate, cover and refrigerate until ready to serve.

To make coconut rice, place rice in fine-mesh sieve, rinse with cold running water and drain well. In wok over medium heat, warm peanut oil for 1 minute. Add onion and stir-fry until softened, about 2 minutes. Add rice, cardamom and water. Bring slowly to boil, reduce heat to very low, cover tightly and cook until rice is tender, 12–14 minutes. Stir in coconut milk and warm water. Turn out on plate, leaving soft rice on bottom of wok. Allow to cool.

Working with one banana leaf square at a time, lay on work surface and spoon 2–3 tablespoons coconut rice in middle. Fold leaf over rice to form parcel. Secure with kitchen string.

Half fill large wok with water (steamer should not touch water) and bring to boil. Working in batches if necessary, arrange parcels in bamboo steamer. Place each fish fillet on square of parchment (baking) paper and arrange fish in steamer. Cover, place steamer in wok and steam until fish flakes when tested with fork, 6–8 minutes, depending on thickness of fillets.

Remove fish and rice parcels from steamer and arrange on individual plates. Top each fish fillet with relish. Coconut rice parcels can be cut in half before serving, or guests can open parcels at table.

Serves 4

FISH FILLETS WITH COCONUT RICE PARCELS

pork

Fried pork in endive

1 tablespoon vegetable oil

2 cloves garlic, crushed

1 tablespoon peeled and grated fresh ginger

6 scallions (shallots/spring onions), chopped

$^1/_2$ teaspoon shrimp paste

1 tablespoon chopped lemongrass

2 teaspoons sambal oelek

7 oz (220 g) pork fillet, finely chopped

8 oz (250 g) cherry tomatoes, quartered

1 tablespoon coconut milk

3 tablespoons chopped fresh cilantro (fresh coriander)

3 heads Belgian endive (chicory/witloof), cored and leaves separated

In wok over medium heat, warm vegetable oil. Add garlic, ginger, scallions, shrimp paste, lemongrass and sambal oelek and stir-fry until aromatic, about 2 minutes. Add pork and cook until pork changes color, about 3 minutes.

Stir in tomatoes and coconut milk and stir-fry until tomatoes soften slightly, 1–2 minutes. Remove from heat and stir in cilantro.

To serve, spoon pork filling into endive leaves. Divide among individual plates and serve hot.

Serves 4

FRIED PORK IN ENDIVE

Pork and nectarine stir-fry

2 tablespoons vegetable oil

3 cloves garlic, crushed

1 small red chili pepper, seeded and chopped

1 lb (500 g) pork fillet, thinly sliced

1 bunch choy sum or spinach, trimmed and cut into
   1¼-in (3-cm) lengths

3 kaffir lime leaves, shredded

2½ tablespoons light soy sauce

2 teaspoons lime juice

2 firm nectarines, pitted and sliced

steamed white rice for serving

In wok over medium-high heat, warm vegetable oil. Add garlic and chili pepper and stir-fry until aromatic, about 1 minute. Add pork, choy sum or spinach and lime leaves and stir-fry until pork changes color, 3–4 minutes. Add soy sauce, lime juice and nectarines and stir-fry until heated through, 1–2 minutes.

Serve hot, accompanied with steamed white rice.

Serves 4–6

Pork and lime patties

8 oz (250 g) ground (minced) pork

2 teaspoons fish sauce

1 teaspoon oyster sauce

2 teaspoons sambal oelek

1 egg white, lightly beaten

2 cloves garlic, crushed

2 tablespoons cornstarch (cornflour)

2 teaspoon grated lime zest

4 kaffir lime leaves, shredded

$^1/_4$ cup (1 oz/30 g) chopped scallions
  (shallots/spring onions)

$^1/_2$ cup (4 fl oz/125 ml) vegetable oil for frying

Thai sweet chili sauce for serving

In bowl, combine pork, fish sauce, oyster sauce, sambal oelek and egg white. Mix well. Add garlic, cornstarch, lime zest, lime leaves and scallions. Using moistened hands, mix until well combined. Divide mixture into 16 pieces and shape into patties.

In wok over medium heat, warm vegetable oil. Working in batches, add pork patties and fry, turning once, until tender and golden on both sides, 6–8 minutes. Drain on paper towels.

Serve hot with Thai sweet chili sauce.

Serves 4

PORK AND LIME PATTIES

Red curry beef

8 oz (250 g) sirloin (rump) or round (topside)
 steak

1 tablespoon vegetable oil

1 tablespoon red curry paste

1 cup (8 fl oz/250 ml) coconut milk

2 teaspoons fish sauce

1 teaspoon palm sugar or brown sugar

1 cup (6 oz/180 g) drained canned baby corn

$1/3$ cup (2 oz/60 g) drained canned straw
 mushrooms

$1/2$ cup ($1/2$ oz/15 g) small fresh basil leaves

steamed white rice for serving

Enclose steak in freezer wrap and freeze until slightly firm, about 30 minutes. Remove from freezer and thinly slice. In wok over medium-high heat, warm oil. Working in batches, add beef and stir-fry until brown, 1–2 minutes. Remove from wok and drain on paper towels. Add curry paste to wok and cook until paste bubbles, 10–15 seconds. Stir in coconut milk, fish sauce, sugar, corn and mushrooms. Bring to boil, reduce heat and simmer, uncovered, for 5 minutes. Add beef and stir-fry until heated through, about 1 minute.

Spoon into bowls and sprinkle each serving with basil leaves. Serve hot, accompanied with steamed white rice.

Serves 4

RED CURRY BEEF

Beef stir-fry with Chinese greens

10½ oz (315 g) sirloin (rump) or round (topside) steak

3 tablespoons vegetable oil

4 cloves garlic, crushed

1 tablespoon peeled and grated fresh ginger

2 small red chili peppers, seeded and chopped

1 bunch Chinese broccoli or 6 celery stalks, trimmed and cut into 1¼-in (3-cm) lengths

7 oz (220 g) sugar snap peas or snow peas (mange-touts), trimmed

3½ oz (105 g) fresh bean sprouts, rinsed

1 tablespoon oyster sauce

1 teaspoon sambal oelek

steamed white rice for serving

Enclose steak in freezer wrap and freeze until slightly firm, about 30 minutes. Remove from freezer and thinly slice. In bowl, combine beef, 1 tablespoon vegetable oil, garlic and ginger. Cover and refrigerate for 30 minutes.

Drain beef from marinade, discarding marinade. In wok over medium-high heat, warm remaining 2 tablespoons vegetable oil. Working in batches, add beef and stir-fry until brown, 1–2 minutes. Remove from wok and drain on paper towels. Add chili pepper, broccoli or celery, sugar snap peas or snow peas and bean sprouts and stir-fry until tender-crisp, 2–3 minutes. Add beef, oyster sauce and sambal oelek. Stir-fry until heated through, about 1 minute.

Serve hot, accompanied with steamed white rice.

Serves 4

Dry beef curry with sweet potato

1 onion, chopped

2 cloves garlic

1 teaspoon shrimp paste

1 teaspoon ground cumin

2 teaspoons ground coriander

1 tablespoon chopped lemongrass

$\frac{1}{2}$ teaspoon ground turmeric

1 teaspoon ground paprika

1 teaspoon grated lime zest

2 tablespoons vegetable oil

11 oz (330 g) sirloin (rump) or round (topside)
   steak, cut into $1\frac{1}{4}$-in (3-cm) cubes

1 cup (8 fl oz/250 ml) water

7 oz (220 g) sweet potato, peeled and finely diced

1 long red chili pepper, seeded and sliced

1 long green chili pepper, seeded and sliced

steamed white rice for serving

Place onion, garlic, shrimp paste, cumin, coriander, lemongrass, turmeric, paprika and lime zest in food processor. Process until smooth. Set aside.

In wok over medium-high heat, warm vegetable oil. Working in batches, add beef and stir-fry until brown, 3–4 minutes. Remove from wok and drain on paper towels. Add spice blend to wok and cook until aromatic, about 1 minute.

Add beef and water and bring to boil. Reduce heat to low, cover and simmer, stirring occasionally, for 30 minutes. Stir in sweet potato and simmer, uncovered, until sweet potato is tender, about 10 minutes. (Add a little more water if necessary.)

To serve, divide among individual plates and sprinkle with sliced chili peppers. Accompany with steamed white rice.

Serves 4

DRY BEEF CURRY WITH SWEET POTATO

duck

Duck with long beans

1 Chinese roast duck

2 teaspoons vegetable oil

4 scallions (shallots/spring onions), chopped

1 tablespoon peeled and shredded fresh ginger

8 long beans, cut into $2\frac{1}{2}$-in (6-cm) lengths

2 tablespoons shredded orange zest

2 tablespoons mirin

$1\frac{1}{2}$ tablespoons light soy sauce

steamed white rice for serving

Cut duck into serving pieces, leaving flesh on bone. Set aside. In wok over medium-high heat, warm vegetable oil. Add scallions and ginger and stir-fry until softened, about 2 minutes. Add beans, orange zest, duck, mirin and soy sauce and stir-fry until heated through, 3–4 minutes.

Serve hot, accompanied with steamed white rice.

Serves 4

Chili chicken and vegetables

2 tablespoons peanut oil

1 small red chili pepper, seeded and finely chopped

5 oz (150 g) skinless chicken breast or thigh fillet,
   cut into 1-in (2.5-cm) cubes

6 asparagus spears, cut into 1¼-in (3-cm) pieces

1 bunch bok choy, trimmed and large leaves halved

4 oz (125 g) sugar snap peas or snow peas
   (mange-touts), trimmed

4 oz (125 g) shittake mushrooms, sliced

¼ cup (2 fl oz/60 ml) chicken broth

2 teaspoons soy sauce

1 tablespoon rice wine

1 teaspoon Asian sesame oil

crisp fried egg noodles for serving (optional)

In wok over medium heat, warm peanut oil. Add chili pepper and chicken and stir-fry until chicken is golden, 4–5 minutes. Raise heat to medium-high, add asparagus, bok choy sugar snap peas or snow peas and mushrooms and stir-fry until vegetables soften slightly, 3–4 minutes. In small bowl, stir together broth, soy sauce, rice wine and sesame oil. Add to wok, reduce heat to medium and cook until heated through.

Serve hot, with crisp fried egg noodles if desired.

Serves 4–6

CHILI CHICKEN AND VEGETABLES

Deep-fried chicken wings

2 teaspoons ground turmeric

1 teaspoon ground chili

2 teaspoons ground coriander

2 teaspoons ground cumin

3 cloves garlic, crushed

12 chicken wings

4 cups (32 fl oz/1 L) vegetable oil for deep frying

Thai sweet chili sauce and lime wedges for serving

In small bowl, combine turmeric, chili, coriander, cumin and garlic. Using hands, rub spices into skin of each chicken wing. Cover and refrigerate for 2 hours.

Heat oil in wok until it reaches 375°F (190°C) on deep-frying thermometer or until small bread cube dropped in oil sizzles and turns golden. Working with one or two wings at a time, add to hot oil and deep-fry until golden brown, 3–4 minutes. Using slotted spoon, remove from wok and drain on paper towels. Keep warm while frying remaining wings.

Serve hot, accompanied with Thai sweet chili sauce for dipping and lime wedges.

Serves 3 or 4

Green chicken curry

2 tablespoon vegetable oil

1 onion, chopped

1 tablespoon green curry paste or to taste

1 lb (500 g) skinless chicken thigh fillets, cut into
thin strips

5 oz (150 g) green beans, trimmed

1³/₄ cups (14 fl oz/440 ml) coconut milk

4 kaffir lime leaves

1 tablespoon fish sauce

1 teaspoon grated lime zest

1 tablespoon lime juice

1 tablespoon brown sugar

2 tablespoons chopped fresh cilantro
(fresh coriander)

steamed white rice for serving

In wok over medium heat, warm vegetable oil. Add onion and curry paste and stir-fry until onion softens, 1–2 minutes. Add chicken and stir-fry until lightly golden, 3–4 minutes. Add beans, coconut milk and lime leaves and bring to boil. Reduce heat to low and simmer, uncovered, until beans are tender-crisp, 3–4 minutes. Add fish sauce, lime zest and juice, sugar and cilantro. Cook for 1 minute.

Serve hot, accompanied with steamed white rice.

Serves 4–6

GREEN CHICKEN CURRY

Crispy wontons with duck

10 scallions (shallots/spring onions), pale portion
   only, cut into 2-in (5-cm) pieces

2 carrots, peeled and julienned

1 Chinese roast duck

6 cups (48 fl oz/1.5 L) vegetable oil for deep-frying

16 wonton wrappers

$1/2$ cup (4 fl oz/125 ml) hoisin sauce

Using sharp knife or scissors, make $1/4$-in (6-mm) cuts into ends of each scallion piece to make fringe. Place scallions and carrots in bowl of ice water. Refrigerate until scallions curl, about 15 minutes.

Remove meat and skin from duck and coarsely chop; discard skin if desired. Heat oil in wok until it reaches 375°F (190°C) on deep-frying thermometer or until small bread cube dropped in oil sizzles and turns golden. Working with one wonton at a time and using two sets of tongs, hold wonton in taco shape and lower into oil. Continue to hold wonton until golden and crisp, about 1 minute. Drain on paper towels. Repeat with remaining wontons.

To serve, fill wontons with scallions, carrots and duck. Drizzle with hoisin sauce and serve immediately.

Serves 4

CRISPY WONTONS WITH DUCK

Chicken chow mein

6 cups (48 fl oz/1.5 L) vegetable oil for deep-
   frying, plus 2 tablespoons oil

6 1/2 oz (200 g) fresh thin egg noodles

3 cloves garlic, crushed

1 tablespoon peeled and grated fresh ginger

1 onion, cut into eighths

1 lb (500 g) skinless chicken thigh fillets, cut into
   3/4-in (2-cm) cubes

1 red bell pepper (capsicum), seeded and sliced

1 green bell pepper (capsicum), seeded and sliced

1 bunch choy sum or spinach, trimmed and cut into
   2-in (5-cm) lengths

3 tablespoons hoisin sauce

1/4 cup (2 fl oz/60 ml) chicken broth mixed with 1
   teaspoon cornstarch (cornflour)

Heat 6 cups (48 fl oz/1.5 L) oil in wok until it reaches 375°F (190°C) on deep-frying thermometer or until small bread cube dropped in oil sizzles and turns golden. Working in small batches, add noodles and fry until golden and crisp, 1–2 minutes. Using slotted spoon, remove from oil and drain on paper towels.

In wok over medium-high heat, warm 2 tablespoons vegetable oil. Add garlic, ginger and onion and stir-fry until onion softens slightly, about 3 minutes. Add chicken and stir-fry until browned, 3–4 minutes. Add bell peppers and choy sum or spinach and stir-fry until tender-crisp, about 2 minutes. Stir in hoisin sauce and broth and cornstarch mixture and cook until sauce boils and thickens slightly, about 2 minutes.

To serve, arrange crisp noodles in nest on serving plates. Top with chicken and vegetables.

Serves 4

CHICKEN CHOW MEIN

Black-eyed pea and sugar snap stir-fry

1 cup (6¹/₂ oz/200 g) dried black-eyed peas (beans)

2 red onions, sliced

juice from 2 lemons

1 tablespoon vegetable oil

2 teaspoons Asian sesame oil

5 oz (150 g) sugar snap peas or snow peas (mange-touts), trimmed

¹/₂ cup (2 oz/60 g) chopped scallions (shallots/spring onions)

1 cup (1 oz/30 g) mint leaves

¹/₂ cup (³/₄ oz/20 g) snipped chives

1 teaspoon fish sauce

1 teaspoon light soy sauce

Place black-eyed peas in large bowl, add cold water to cover, cover and allow to stand overnight. Drain and rinse peas and place in saucepan with plenty of water to cover. Bring to boil, reduce heat to low and simmer, uncovered, until tender, about 1 hour. Drain and allow to cool completely.

In bowl, combine onions and lemon juice, cover and allow to stand for 1 hour.

In wok over medium-high heat, warm vegetable and sesame oils. Add sugar snap peas or snow peas and stir-fry until tender-crisp, about 2 minutes. Remove from heat and allow to cool completely. Add black-eyed peas and sugar snap peas or snow peas to bowl with onions. Add scallions, mint, chives, fish sauce and soy sauce. Mix well, cover and refrigerate for 30 minutes.

Serve chilled.

Serves 4

Butternut squash and lentil salad

DRESSING

$^1/_3$ cup (3 fl oz/90 ml) olive oil

2 teaspoons grated lime zest

$^1/_3$ cup (3 fl oz/90 ml) lime juice

2 tablespoons chopped fresh cilantro (fresh coriander)

$^1/_2$ teaspoon superfine (caster) sugar

ground pepper to taste

SALAD

1 butternut squash (pumpkin), about 1 lb (500 g), peeled and cut into $1^1/_2$-in (4-cm) cubes

$^1/_2$ cup ($3^1/_2$ oz/105 g) dried red lentils

1 tablespoon vegetable oil

1 small red chili pepper, seeded and chopped

1 teaspoon cumin seeds

2 teaspoons coriander seeds, cracked

To make dressing, place olive oil, lime zest and juice, cilantro, sugar and pepper in screw-top jar. Shake well to combine.

Line large steamer with parchment (baking) paper. Half fill wok with water (steamer should not touch water) and bring to boil. Place squash cubes in steamer, cover and place steamer over boiling water. Steam until squash cubes are tender but retain their shape, 10–12 minutes. Add more water to wok when necessary. Remove steamer from wok and allow pumpkin to cool.

Place lentils in saucepan with water to cover. Bring to boil and cook until tender (do not overcook), about 5 minutes. Drain and allow to cool.

In wok over medium-high heat, warm vegetable oil. Add chili pepper and cumin and coriander seeds and cook until aromatic, 1–2 minutes. Add squash and lentils and stir-fry until flavors are blended, about 1 minute. Remove from heat and stir in dressing. Mix well

Serve warm or refrigerate for 30 minutes and serve chilled.

Serves 4

Tofu and vegetable stir-fry

¹/₃ cup (3 fl oz/90 ml) vegetable oil

6¹/₂ oz (200 g) firm tofu, cut into 1-in (2.5-cm) cubes

3 cloves garlic, crushed

2 teaspoons peeled and grated fresh ginger

2 onions, cut into eighths

1 bunch Chinese broccoli, trimmed and cut into 1¹/₂-in (4-cm) lengths

3¹/₂ oz (105 g) snow peas (mange-touts), trimmed and sliced crosswise

1 red bell pepper (capsicum), seeded and sliced

1 cup (6 oz/180 g) drained canned baby corn

1 bunch bok choy, trimmed and cut into 1¹/₂-in (4-cm) lengths, or 1 bunch spinach, trimmed

2 tablespoons oyster sauce

1 tablespoon light soy sauce

steamed white rice for serving

In wok over medium heat, warm vegetable oil. Working in batches, add tofu and stir-fry until golden on all sides, 2–3 minutes. Using slotted spoon, remove from wok and drain on paper towels. Pour off all but 2 tablespoons oil from wok and return to medium heat. Add garlic, ginger and onions and stir-fry until softened, 2–3 minutes. Add broccoli, snow peas, bell pepper, corn and bok choy or spinach. Stir-fry until vegetables are tender-crisp, 3–4 minutes. Add tofu and oyster and soy sauces and gently stir-fry until heated through, 1–2 minutes.

Serve hot, accompanied with steamed white rice.

Serves 4

TOFU AND VEGETABLE STIR-FRY

Bell peppers and mushrooms with noodles

5 oz (150 g) fresh egg noodles

6 Chinese dried mushrooms

1 tablespoon vegetable oil

1 teaspoon Asian sesame oil

1 red bell pepper (capsicum), seeded and sliced

1 yellow bell pepper (capsicum), seeded and sliced

1 cup (4 oz/125 g) fresh bean sprouts, rinsed

4 oz (125 g) fresh shittake mushrooms, sliced

4 oz (125 g) fresh oyster mushrooms, sliced if large

$^1/_4$ cup (2 fl oz/60 ml) Thai sweet chili sauce

1 tablespoon light soy sauce

$^1/_4$ cup ($^1/_4$ oz/7 g) fresh cilantro (fresh coriander) leaves

Bring saucepan of water to boil. Add noodles and cook until tender, about 3 minutes. Drain and set aside.

Place dried mushrooms in small bowl, add boiling water to cover and allow to stand until softened, 10–15 minutes. Drain and squeeze out excess liquid. Thinly slice mushrooms, discarding thick stems.

In wok over medium heat, warm vegetable and sesame oils. Add bell peppers, bean sprouts and fresh mushrooms and stir-fry until slightly softened, 1–2 minutes. Add noodles, reconstituted mushrooms and chili and soy sauces and stir-fry until heated through, 2–3 minutes.

Serve hot, garnished with cilantro leaves.

Serves 4

Steamed vegetable buns

DOUGH

1 package ($^1/_4$ oz/7 g) active dry yeast

$^1/_2$ cup (4 fl oz/125 ml) warm water

$^1/_4$ cup superfine (caster) sugar

1 cup (5 oz/150 g) all-purpose (plain) flour

$^1/_2$ cup ($2^1/_2$ oz/75 g) self-rising flour

1 tablespoon butter, melted

FILLING

2 Chinese dried mushrooms

2 teaspoons Asian sesame oil

$^1/_2$ small leek, chopped

2 cloves garlic, crushed

1 teaspoon peeled and grated fresh ginger

2 oz (60 g) firm tofu, chopped

1 tablespoon lime juice

$^1/_2$ small carrot, peeled and grated

1 tablespoon chopped roasted cashew nuts

2 teaspoons Thai sweet chili sauce

1 tablespoon chopped fresh mint

2 teaspoons hot bean paste

3 teaspoons tomato paste

soy sauce and chili oil for serving

To make dough, in small bowl, combine yeast and 2 tablespoons of warm water, 1 teaspoon of sugar and 1 teaspoon of all-purpose flour. Mix until well combined. Cover and allow to stand in warm place until frothy, about 15 minutes. Sift remaining all-purpose flour and self-rising flour into large bowl. Add remaining sugar, yeast mixture and remaining warm water. Using wooden spoon, mix to form soft dough. Turn dough out onto floured work surface. Knead until dough is smooth and elastic, 3–5 minutes. Place dough in large oiled bowl, cover and let stand in warm place until dough is doubled in bulk.

To make filling, place dried mushrooms in small bowl, add boiling water to cover and allow to stand until softened, 10–15 minutes. Drain and squeeze out excess liquid. Thinly slice mushrooms, discarding thick stems. In wok over medium heat, warm sesame oil. Add leek, garlic and ginger and stir-fry until leek softens, about 2 minutes. Stir in tofu, lime juice, carrot, cashews, chili sauce, mint and bean and tomato pastes. Stir-fry until heated through, about 1 minute. Remove from heat and mix well. Allow to cool completely.

Punch down dough. Turn out onto floured work surface and knead until smooth, about 5 minutes. Divide dough into 16 pieces. Roll or press each to form 2½-in (6-cm) circle. Cover circles with damp kitchen towel to prevent them from drying out. Working with one circle at a time, lay it on work surface and place 2 teaspoons filling in middle. Gather edges together and twist to seal. Set aside, covered with damp kitchen towel. Repeat with remaining dough.

Cut 16 squares of parchment (baking) paper and place under each bun. Half fill wok with water (steamer should not touch water) and bring to boil. Working in batches, arrange buns in steamer, cover and place steamer over boiling water. Steam for 10 minutes, adding more water to wok when necessary. Remove steamer from wok and carefully remove buns from steamer.

Serve warm with soy sauce and chili oil for dipping.

Serves 4

desserts

Lime and coconut pudding with lime-ginger syrup

PUDDING

$^3/_4$ cup (6 oz/180 g) butter

$^1/_3$ cup (3 oz/90 g) superfine (caster) sugar

1 teaspoon grated lime zest

1 teaspoon vanilla extract (essence)

3 eggs

1 cup (5 oz/150 g) self-rising flour, sifted

1 cup (4 oz/125 g) unsweetened shredded
   (desiccated) coconut

SYRUP

$^1/_2$ cup (4 oz/125 g) decorating (crystal) sugar

3 tablespoons lime juice

1 tablespoon shredded lime zest

1 tablespoon peeled and shredded fresh ginger

whipped cream for serving

Butter six ½ cup (4 fl oz/125 ml) ramekins and line bottoms with parchment (baking) paper. Set aside. To make pudding, place butter, sugar and lime zest in bowl. Using electric mixer, beat until light and creamy, 3–4 minutes. Add vanilla. Add eggs, one at a time, beating well after each addition. If mixture begins to curdle, add 1 tablespoon all-purpose (plain) flour. Fold in flour and coconut and mix well.

Spoon pudding into prepared ramekins. Cover each with piece of buttered parchment paper. Half fill wok with water (steamer should not touch water) and bring water to boil. Arrange ramekins in steamer, cover and place steamer over boiling water. Steam until puddings are firm to touch, 40–45 minutes. Add more water to wok when necessary.

To make syrup, place sugar, lime juice and zest and ginger in small saucepan over low heat. Stir until sugar dissolves. Bring to boil and allow to boil for 2 minutes. Remove from heat.

Slowly pour warm syrup over warm puddings. Serve, garnished with whipped cream.

Serves 6

Spicy fruit salad

1¼ cups (10 fl oz/300 ml) water

½ cup (4 oz/125 g) decorating (crystal) sugar

juice and zest of 1 orange

3 star anise

6 whole black peppercorns

6 whole cardamom pods

3 cinnamon sticks

3 peaches, peeled, pitted and sliced

4 fresh figs, quartered

1½ cups (6½ oz/200 g) blueberries

2 oranges, peeled and cut into segments

Combine water, sugar, orange zest and juice, star anise, peppercorns, cardamom and cinnamon in wok. Place over low heat and stir until sugar dissolves.

Raise heat to medium and bring to boil. Reduce heat to low and simmer, uncovered, for 10 minutes. Remove from heat.

Add peaches, figs, blueberries and oranges.

Allow to cool to room temperature and serve warm or refrigerate for 30 minutes and serve chilled.

Serves 4

SPICY FRUIT SALAD

Polenta pudding with mango sauce

PUDDING

$1/2$ cup (4 oz/125 g) butter

$2/3$ cup (5 oz/150 g) sugar

2 teaspoons grated lemon zest

2 eggs

1 cup (5 oz/150 g) self-rising flour

$1/2$ teaspoon baking powder

$1/4$ teaspoon salt

$2/3$ cup ($3^{1}/_{2}$ oz/105 g) polenta

$1/2$ cup (4 fl oz/125 ml) sour cream

$1/3$ cup (3 fl oz/90 ml) milk

MANGO SAUCE

2 mangos, peeled, pitted and sliced

2 tablespoons confectioners' (icing) sugar

2 tablespoons lime juice

1 teaspoon grated lime zest

Butter six $1/2$ cup (4 fl oz/125 ml) ramekins and line bottoms with parchment (baking) paper. Set aside.

To make puddings, place butter, sugar and lemon zest in bowl. Using electric mixer, beat until light and creamy, 3–4 minutes. Add eggs, one at a time, beating well after each addition. If mixture begins to curdle, add 1 tablespoon all-purpose (plain) flour.

Sift flour, baking powder and salt into bowl. Stir in polenta. Combine sour cream and milk. Fold flour mixture into egg mixture alternately with sour cream mixture. Mix well.

Spoon pudding into prepared ramekins. Cover each with piece of buttered parchment paper. Half fill wok with water (steamer should not touch water) and bring water to boil. Arrange ramekins in steamer, cover and place steamer over boiling water. Steam until puddings are firm to touch, 45–50 minutes. Add more water to wok when necessary.

To make mango sauce, place mangos, sugar and lime juice and zest in food processor. Process until smooth.

Remove steamer from wok and carefully remove ramekins from steamer. Run sharp knife around sides of each ramekin. Invert onto plate and unmold pudding. Serve warm with mango sauce.

Makes 6

Rose water doughnuts

YOGURT SAUCE

6¹/₂ oz (200 g) plain (natural) yogurt

3 teaspoons rose water

1 tablespoon confectioners' (icing) sugar, sifted

DOUGHNUTS

2¹/₄ cups (11 oz/330 g) self-rising flour, sifted

¹/₂ cup (2 oz/60 g) ground almonds

¹/₃ cup (3 oz/90 g) butter or ghee, plus 2 cups
    (16 fl oz/500 ml) vegetable oil or ghee for
    deep-frying

¹/₃ cup (3 fl oz/90 ml) plain (natural) yogurt

¹/₄ cup (2 fl oz/60 ml) warm water

2 teaspoons rose water

grated zest of 1 orange

¹/₃ cup (2¹/₂ oz/75 g) superfine (caster) sugar

To make yogurt sauce, in small bowl, combine yogurt, rose water and sugar. Mix well. Cover and refrigerate until ready to serve.

To make doughnuts, in bowl, combine flour and almonds. Using fingertips, rub ⅓ cup (3 oz/90m g) butter or ghee into flour. Stir in yogurt, warm water, rose water and orange zest. Mix to form soft dough. Turn out onto floured work surface. Knead until smooth, about 2 minutes. Divide dough into 30 pieces. Roll each into ball.

Heat 2 cups (16 fl oz/500 ml) vegetable oil or ghee in wok until it reaches 375°F (190°C) on deep-frying thermometer or until small bread cube dropped into liquid sizzles and turns golden. Working in batches, add doughnuts and deep-fry until golden, 5–6 minutes. Using slotted spoon, remove from wok and drain on paper towels. Place superfine sugar on plate and roll each doughnut in sugar until well coated. Serve warm with yogurt sauce.

Makes 30 doughnuts

ROSE WATER DOUGHNUTS

Glossary

Asian sesame oil. Dark- or golden-colored oil extracted from sesame seeds, which give it a satisfying nutty flavor.

bamboo shoots. Young shoots of a plant with a mildly sweet flavor and crunchy texture. Boiled before used in cooking, they are commonly found canned, packed in water.

banana leaves. Large leaves from the banana plant, whose pliable texture allows them to be used for wrapping foods before they are steamed. Parchment (baking) paper can be substituted.

bean sprouts. Sprouting green mung beans, sold fresh or canned. Fresh sprouts tend to have a crisper texture and a more delicate flavor. Store in refrigerator for up to 3 days.

bok choy. Asian variety of cabbage with thick white stalks and mild-flavored dark green leaves. Sizes of bunches vary, from longer than celery stalks to baby bok choy about 6 inches (15 cm) long. Also known as Chinese cabbage. If unavailable, use Chinese broccoli or choy sum.

cellophane noodles. Thin translucent dried noodles made from mung bean starch and sold in bundles. Also called bean thread noodles.

chili oil. Spicy oil produced by steeping dried red chili peppers in oil. Use this hot oil only by the drop. Store in refrigerator after opening.

chili paste. Fiery condiment containing ground dried or fresh chili peppers and sometimes garlic and ginger, depending on the country of origin.

Chinese barbecue pork. Boneless pork that has been marinated in Chinese five-spice powder and soy sauce and then roasted. Sold in slices or strips in Chinese markets. Store up to 2 days in refrigerator.

Chinese broccoli. Bitter-tasting broccoli with white flowers. Also known as gai laan. Chinese broccoli and choy sum can be used in place of each other.

Chinese dried mushrooms. Intensely flavorful, dark mushrooms that need to be rehydrated before use. Soak, off heat, in boiling water for 10-15 minutes and squeeze dry before slicing or chopping; discard tough stems.

Chinese roast duck. Sold freshly roasted in Chinese markets and delicious in stir-fries or on its own. Use 1–2 days after purchase. Substitute roast chicken if unavailable.

choy sum. Popular and widely available Chinese green with yellow flowers and thin stalks. Every part of the mild-flavored vegetable can be used. Also known as flowering cabbage.

cilantro. Pungent, fragrant leaves from the coriander plant, resembling parsley and also called Chinese parsley and fresh coriander. An herb used widely in Southeast Asian cuisine.

coconut milk. Rich liquid extracted from shredded coconut that has been steeped in water. It is used in sweet and savory Asian dishes. Coconut milk is available canned.

curry paste. Condiment consisting of curry seasonings and red or green chili peppers. Both red curry paste and green curry paste are available bottled. Store in refrigerator after opening.

fish sauce. Pungent sauce of salted fermented fish and other seasonings. Products vary in intensity depending on the country of origin. Fish sauce from Thailand, called nam pla, is a commonly available variety.

garam masala. Hot to mild mixture of ground spices used widely in Indian cooking. The combination, which varies depending on the region of origin and the intended use, often includes cinnamon, black pepper, coriander, cumin, cardamom, cloves and nutmeg. Garam masala blends may be custom-ground from whole spices or purchased already ground.

ghee. Butter from which milk solids have been removed. Used to give a rich, buttery taste to curries. To make ghee, or clarified butter, place 1 lb (500 g) unsalted butter in heavy-bottomed saucepan over low heat. Melt butter and gently simmer until moisture evaporates and milk solids separate from clear butter fat; stir constantly to prevent browning. Remove from heat and strain through double layer of cheesecloth (muslin). Allow to cool and refrigerate until ready to use.

ginger. Thick rootlike rhizome of the ginger plant, with a sharp, pungent flavor. Once the thin tan skin is peeled from fresh ginger, the flesh is grated or sliced. Store fresh ginger in refrigerator for 2–3 days.

glutinous rice. Generally white and sometimes dark rice that cooks to a sticky mass rather than separate grains. Also called sticky rice.

hoisin sauce. Sweet, thick Chinese sauce made from soybeans and also containing vinegar, sugar, chili peppers and other seasonings. Bottled hoisin can be stored indefinitely in refrigerator.

hot bean paste. Hot, thick, red-brown sauce made from fermented soybeans, chili peppers, garlic and spices. Sometimes called red bean paste or chili bean paste.

jasmine rice. Aromatic long-grain rice popular in Thai cooking.

kaffir lime leaves. Leaves from the kaffir lime tree generally used dried but also fresh to add an enticing citrus flavor and aroma to soups, curries and other simmered dishes.

lemongrass. Tropical grass whose pale stalks lend an intense lemon flavor to Southeast Asian dishes. Wrapped in a damp kitchen towel, lemongrass can be refrigerated for up to 1 month. The stalks, trimmed of the green blades, are bruised or chopped before use. Substitute grated lemon zest if lemongrass is unavailable.

long bean. Related to the black-eyed pea and also called yard-long bean, though most beans found in markets are 24 inches (60 cm) or less in length. The thin, flexible but firm-textured green beans are cut into short lengths before they are cooked.

mirin. Sweet alcoholic wine made from rice and used in Japanese cooking. Sweet sherry can be substituted.

miso. Thick paste of fermented ground soybeans, used in Japanese soups and other dishes. Light-colored varieties of miso are milder in flavor than dark-colored pastes.

oyster mushrooms. Creamy white mushrooms with fan-shaped caps, named for their resemblance to an oyster. Possessing a mild flavor, oyster mushrooms grow in the wild and are cultivated. Substitute button mushrooms if unavailable.

oyster sauce. Thick, dark brown Chinese sauce made from fermented dried oysters and soy sauce and used to impart an intense or mild briny flavor to stir-fries and other dishes. Store in refrigerator after opening.

palm sugar. Dense, heavy, dark cakes made from the sap of palm trees and sold in Asian markets. Shave with a sharp knife or grate before using. Substitute brown sugar if unavailable.

rice vinegar. Mildly piquant vinegar produced from fermented rice. Japanese and Chinese vinegars can be found in Asian markets and well-stocked food stores.

rice wine. Sweet, low-alcohol Chinese wine, also known as shaoxing wine or shaoxing yellow rice wine, made from fermented glutinous rice. Sake or dry sherry can be substituted.

sambal oelek. Spicy Indonesian paste consisting of ground chili peppers combined with salt and occasionally vinegar. It can be used as a substitute for fresh chili peppers.

shiitake mushrooms. Meaty mushrooms with light or dark brown caps. Dried shiitakes, also available, need to be rehydrated. Soak, off heat, in boiling water for 10-15 minutes and squeeze dry before slicing or chopping.

shrimp paste. Produced by drying, salting and pounding shrimp into a pungent-flavored paste that is then formed into blocks or cakes.

soy sauce. Salty sauce made from fermented soybeans and usually wheat, used as an ingredient and as a table condiment. Dark soy sauce is thicker and often less salty than light soy sauce. Low-sodium products are also available.

spring roll wrappers. Thin sheets of rice flour dough, used to enclose savory fillings. Sometimes called spring roll skins.

straw mushrooms. Small mushrooms possessing rounded caps and lacking stems. Because the fresh mushrooms easily lose their earthy taste, straw mushrooms are best purchased canned, packed in water.

Thai sweet chili sauce. Mild, sweet chili sauce used as a flavoring and as a dipping sauce. Store in refrigerator after opening.

tofu. Produced from soybeans that have been dried, soaked, cooked, puréed and pressed to form cakes or squares that range in texture from soft to firm. Mild in flavor, tofu readily absorbs the seasonings of the preparations in which it is used.

udon noodles. Soft, creamy white, Japanese wheat flour noodle, available fresh or dried and in a variety of widths.

water chestnut. Tuber of a plant grown in Asia, round in shape with subtly sweet, crunchy, light-colored flesh. Water chestnuts are widely available canned; after opening, store in clean water in the refrigerator for up to 3 weeks. Also known as horses' hooves.

wonton wrapper. Thin sheets of wheat-based or egg-based dough, square or circular in shape, used to enclose a variety of fillings. Available fresh or frozen. Also called wonton skins or dumpling wrappers.

Index

Arugula pesto 58

Beans, black-eyed, and sugar-snap
    stir-fry 88
Beef
    dry curry with sweet potato 74
    red curry 70
    stir-fry with Chinese greens 72
Beer-battered prawns with mango
    salsa 14
Bell peppers and mushrooms with
    noodles 94
Black-eyed pea and sugar snap stir-
    fry 88
Braised shrimp in ginger-coconut
    sauce 52
Buns, steamed vegetable 96
Butternut squash and lentil salad 90

Capsicums (bell peppers) and
    mushrooms with noodles 94
Carrot, coconut and ginger soup 30
Chicken
    broth with dumplings 34
    chow mein 86
    fried wontons 26
    green curry 82
    and mushroom soup 36
    and vegetables, chili 78
Chicken wings, deep fried 80
Chili chicken and vegetables 78

Chili fried rice 42
Chow mein, chicken 86
Cilantro
    shrimp toasts 24
    tomato relish 62
Coconut
    carrot and ginger soup 30
    and ginger rice 50
    and lime pudding with lime-ginger
        syrup 98
    rice parcels 62
    and vegetable soup 28
Coriander *see* Cilantro
Crab mini spring rolls 22
Crispy wontons with duck 84
Curry
    dry beef, with sweet potato 74
    green chicken 82
    red beef 70

Deep-fried chicken wings 80
Dipping sauce 22
Doughnuts, rose water 104
Dressing, grapefruit 18
Dry beef curry with sweet potato 74
Duck
    with crispy wontons 84
    with long beans 76
Dumplings
    with chicken broth 34
    steamed shrimp 20

Endive, fried pork in 64

Fish
    fillets with coconut rice parcels and
        cilantro-tomato relish 62
    spicy snapper with parsnip
        chips 56
Fried chicken wontons 26
Fried noodles with pork 44
Fried pork in endive 64
Fruit salad, spicy 100

Ginger-coconut rice 50
Grapefruit dressing 18
Green chicken curry 82

Laksa, salmon 46
Lentil and butternut squash
    salad 90
Lime and coconut pudding with lime-
    ginger syrup 98

Mango
    salsa 14
    sauce 102
Mini crab spring rolls 22
Miso with scallops and ginger 32
Mushrooms
    and bell peppers with
        noodles 94
    and chicken soup 36

Nasi goreng 38
Noodles
    with baked vegetables 48
    with bell peppers and mushrooms 94
    fried, with pork 44

Octopus, stir-fried, with long beans and snow peas 54

Patties, pork and lime 68
Peanut and chili bundles 16
Peas, black-eyed, and sugar snap stir-fry 88
Polenta pudding with mango sauce 102
Pork
    fried, in endive 64
    with fried noodles 44
    and lime patties 68
    and nectarine stir-fry 66
    and rice steamed balls 40
Prawns see Shrimp
Pudding
    lime and coconut, with lime-ginger syrup 98
    polenta, with mango sauce 102

Red curry beef 70
Relish, cilantro-tomato 62
Rice
    chili fried 42
    coconut parcels 62
    ginger-coconut 50
    nasi goreng 38
    and pork steamed balls 40

Rocket (arugula) pesto 58
Rose water doughnuts 104

Salad
    butternut squash and lentil 90
    shrimp and avocado, with crispy wontons 18
Salmon laksa 46
Salsa, mango 14
Scallops
    with arugula pesto and sweet potato purÈe 58
    and ginger with miso 32
Shrimp
    and avocado salad with crispy wontons 18
    beer-battered, with mango salsa 14
    cilantro toasts 24
    steamed dumplings 20
    stir-fried chili-lime 60
Snapper, spicy, with parsnip chips 56
Soup
    carrot, coconut and ginger 30
    chicken broth with dumplings 34
    coconut and vegetable 28
    miso with scallops and ginger 32
    mushroom and chicken 36
    salmon laksa 46
Spicy fruit salad 100
Spicy snapper with parsnip chips 56
Spring rolls, mini crab 22
Squash and lentil salad 90
Squid, stir-fried, with long beans and snow peas 54
Steamed rice-and-pork balls 40

Steamed shrimp dumplings 20
Steamed vegetable buns 96
Stir-fried chili-lime shrimp 60
Stir-fried octopus with long beans and snow peas 54
Sugar snap and black-eyed pea stir-fry 88

Toasts, cilantro shrimp 24
Tofu, and vegetable stir-fry 92
Tomato-cilantro relish 62

Vegetables
    baked, with noodles 48
    and coconut soup 28
    steamed buns 96
    and tofu stir-fry 92

Wontons
crispy, with duck 84
crispy, with shrimp and avocado salad 18
fried chicken 26
peanut and chili bundles 16

Yogurt sauce 104

Guide to weights and measures

The conversions given in the recipes in this book are approximate. Whichever system you choose, the important thing to remember is to ensure the balance remains the same thoughout the ingredients. If you follow all the metric measures you will end up with the same proportions as if you followed all the imperial.

DRY MEASURES

Imperial	Metric
$^1/_6$ oz	5 g
$^1/_2$ oz	15 g
1 oz	30 g
2 oz	60 g
3 oz	90 g
$3^1/_2$ oz	100 g
4 oz ($^1/_4$ lb)	125 g
5 oz	150 g
6 oz	180 g
$6^1/_2$ oz	200 g
7 oz	220 g
8 oz ($^1/_2$ lb)	250 g
9 oz	280 g
10 oz	300 g
11 oz	330 g
12 oz ($^3/_4$ lb)	375 g
13 oz	400 g
14 oz	440 g
15 oz	470 g
16 oz (1 lb)	500 g
24 oz ($1^1/_2$ lb)	750 g
32 oz (2 lb)	1 kg
3 lb	1.5 kg
4 lb	2 kg

USEFUL CONVERSIONS

$^1/_4$ teaspoon	1.25 ml
$^1/_2$ teaspoon	2.5 ml
1 teaspoon	5 ml
1 Australian tablespoon	20 ml (4 teaspoons)
1 UK/US tablespoon	15 ml (3 teaspoons)

Butter/Shortening

1 tablespoon	$^1/_2$ oz	15 g
$1^1/_2$ tablespoons	$^3/_4$ oz	20 g
2 tablespoons	1 oz	30 g
3 tablespoons	$1^1/_2$ oz	50 g

OVEN TEMPERATURE GUIDE

Oven description	°C	°F	Gas Mark
Cool	100	200	$^1/_4$
Very slow	120	250	$^1/_2$
Slow	150	300	2
Warm	160	325	3
Moderate	180	350	4
Moderately hot	190	375	5
Moderately hot	200	400	6
Hot	220	425	7
Very hot	230	450	8
Extremely hot	250	500	10

LIQUID MEASURES

Imperial	Metric	Cup
1 fl oz	30 ml	
2 fl oz	60 ml	$^1/_4$ cup
3 fl oz	90 ml	$^1/_3$ cup
4 fl oz	125 ml	$^1/_2$ cup
5 fl oz	150 ml	$^2/_3$ cup
6 fl oz	180 ml	$^3/_4$ cup
8 fl oz	250 ml	1 cup
10 fl oz	300 ml	$1^1/_2$ cups
14 oz	450 ml	2 cups
16 fl oz	500 ml	2 cups
24 fl oz	750 ml	3 cups
32 fl oz	1000 ml (1 litre)	4 cups

Published by TIME-LIFE BOOKS, LONDON

TIME-LIFE IS A TRADEMARK OF TIME WARNER INC. USA

Publisher: Deborah Nixon
Production Manager: Sally Stokes
Project Co-ordinator: Jenny Coren
Editor: Judith Dunham
Design Concepts: Kerry Klinner
Photographer: Louise Lister
Stylist: Vicki Liley

ISBN 0 7054 30553

Set in Frutiger on QuarkXPress
Printed in Tien Wah Press (Pte) Ltd by Singapore

Thanks to:
Country Floors, Woollahra
Made in Japan, Newtown
Orson & Blake, Woollahra
The Bay Tree, Woollahra
Mrs Red & Sons, Surry Hills